FROM
UK TO BELGIUM
AND BACK

FROM
UK TO BELGIUM
AND BACK

A collection of anecdotes, memories and short tales

Mark Harland

© Mark Harland 2020

Published by MVH Publishing 2020

A CIP catalogue record for this book is available from the British Library.

ISBN 978-0-9935895-4-6 (Paperback)
ISBN 978-0-9935895-5-3 (ePub)
ISBN 978-0-9935895-6-0 (Mobi)

Book layout by Clare Brayshaw

Prepared and printed by:

York Publishing Services Ltd
64 Hallfield Road
Layerthorpe
York
YO31 7ZQ

Tel: 01904 431213

Website: www.yps-publishing.co.uk

FOREWORD

I have to admit it. I was not overly excited at the invitation. To me Belgium epitomised boring flat land, war cemeteries and the European Union.

'I'm going to Belgium next week with Pat and Jonesy. Do you fancy coming with us? It's always a good craic, I promise you.'

So spoke my good friend Terry McMahon, a former colleague and friend of my father Victor. There was only one reason Terry was going to Belgium and that was his love affair with Golden Virginia tobacco which sold in that neck of the woods for about a third of the price in the UK.

That evening I went to visit Dad in the Rambla Nursing Home in Scarborough where he had been resident for almost a year. He relied on my daily visits to keep his spirits up (usually rum) but to be fair I enjoyed them too. We were mates as well as father and son.

'I'll be fine. Your mother and I used to love going to Belgium on the ferry from Harwich to Ostend. She loved Bruges too. Somewhere in the house are some crystal liquer glasses which we bought in Bruges. Britain has a special relationship with the Belgians – and don't forget you have some Flemish blood in you. My Mother's maiden name was Collard and they left Flanders for London in the late

Nineteenth century with much of the flax industry. You just go, Boy. Like I said, I'll be fine.'

And so began my own love affair. Not with Golden Virginia but with a lovely part of the world full of friendly, generous and hospitable people.

A week later, the 29th January 2003 to be precise, I embarked on the P & O ferry mv *Pride of Bruges* at King George Docks in Hull. I could not in my wildest dreams have envisaged that this would be the first of over sixty such trips. My life has never been quite the same since.

Mark Harland

1.

THE WEATHER FORECAST

Bing bong! The ship's Tannoy brought everybody immediately to attention and the Dutch Master's tones were clear and soothing, like verbal Advocaat.

'Good evening, my name is Arri van Gelder, your Captain, shpeaking to you from the bridge. Just to let you know that the *Pride of Bruges* is now ready for sea and we will be leaving the berth in a few minutsh time. The wedder forecash is for moderate eashterly windsh, backing north easht. Sea state is moderate to rough. So take care when moving around the ship. We expect to be on the berth in Zeebrugge tomorrow morning at eight forty-five Continental Time. On behalf of P and O I wish you a pleasant crosshing.'

I was all ears. It was over thirty years since I had been on a large boat – the ss *Orsova* of P & O Orient Lines. Surely this North Sea ferry couldn't live up to the pedigree of the iconic company that epitomised the cream of the British Merchant Marine. Could it?

The thirty thousand ton ferry (I couldn't believe how big it was) slipped its moorings and inched, or even centimetered, forward. It had barely travelled twice its own length before it spun dramatically to starboard and headed for the entrance to the lock which it would have to navigate before it could enter the River Humber en route to the North Sea. I wanted to go out on deck but it was dark and the weather unpleasant so I stayed in the Sunset Lounge with Terry, Pat and Jonesy. The last two were in their early eighties and laughing and drinking beer, no doubt feeling liberated from the normal presence of their wives. I was by far the youngest as I had yet to celebrate my fiftieth.

The beer flowed like Niagara Falls at a price below normal pub prices. A holiday atmosphere was already in the air. I gave my Dad a quick call on my mobile, fearful that the signal would be lost as soon as we reached the open sea.

'Have a drink with me and your Mum, Boy, in Bruges won't you?'

Mum had passed away a decade earlier but a lump still came into my throat. I felt a little guilty not taking Dad with me but his emphysema and limited mobility would have made it very tricky for him. There was another forbear I wanted to take a drink with as well but breakfast time the following day was not, to put it mildly, the time to raise a glass.

As a little thank you for organising the trip and the tickets, I took Terry to the *Four Seasons* restaurant which operated on a self-service buffet system. It was busy and the fare on offer was well presented and tasty. Washed down with beer and accompanied by numerous roll-up fags (for Terry) all was well with the world. You could still smoke in restaurants in those days.

After supper we rejoined Pat and Jonesy who amazingly were still drinking beer. I was surprised when an Entertainments Officer came over the microphone and announced that the on-board resident duo would soon start. I can't remember their names but a girl sang and a guy played keyboards.

'Any requests?' was met by a loud 'Bluebells over the white cliffs of Dover' by a now three sheets to the wind Terry despite the fact the ship was propelled by four giant marine diesels and not sails. Two hundred people laughed and Terry lit another roll-up. Once past Spurn Point the sheltered waters of the estuary were left behind and the correctly forecast easterly caused the ship, on a south easterly bearing, to roll more than a bit. It didn't bother me at all. As my father had once said to me 'You can't beat a bit of rough weather for keeping the queue down at the bar.' Not that there was a queue anyway. Stewards seemed to be everywhere.

At about midnight GMT we repaired to our cabins for the night. The top bunk was my allotted station which suited me just fine. The motion of the ship gently rocked me to sleep and I think my last conscious thoughts were of the old P & O mantra of 'POSH' – denoting port out, starboard home. In the days before air-conditioning this was a reminder for passengers travelling to join the British Raj in India to select a cabin on the port, and thus cooler, side of a ship for the outward voyage and the opposite when homeward bound. Our port-side cabin was also booked for the return journey so it was 'POPH' which doesn't quite have the same ring to it – does it?

Bing bong! 'Good morning ladies and gentlemen.' The Tannoy system was in good voice.

'The time is seven o' clock Continental Time and breakfast is now being served in the Four Seasons Restaurant.'

I switched on my light and looked at my watch. It read six o'clock. Oh heck, of course, I had forgotten to put my watch one hour forward. I was still on GMT – or Zulu as my Dad called it in his non PC vernacular. I remedied that error instantly. With the ship still rocking I took care to arrive at carpet level in one piece and entered the en-suite bathroom to ablute, shave and 'put my eyes in' as I always described my contact lenses. We had an 'outside' cabin and I peaked out through the gap in the curtain. It was pitch black but I could make out some lights in the distance which I guessed were the Port of Zeebrugge. I left Terry asleep and headed for the restaurant which was on the same deck.

Hardly anyone else was eating breakfast and to be truthful I wasn't really hungry. I ate sausages, eggs and toast and then made my way up three further decks until I found myself on a weather deck – that means outside to you non-maritime types. I climbed up a ladder to the boat deck just as the *Pride of Bruges* passed between the red and green lights marking the harbour entrance. It was a poignant moment for me.

'Hi Grandpop! I finally made it to Zeebrugge. I'll raise my glass to you later. Promise.'

Almost eighty-five years earlier, my paternal Grandfather Clement, an Electrical Artificer (First Class) had been on the daring Zeebrugge Raid. Zeebrugge, and further inland Bruges, had been German U-boat bases and the Raid was an attempt to block the entrance by blowing up merchant ships loaded with explosives. Many were killed and more Victoria Crosses were awarded that day since the notorious Rorke's Drift in the Zulu War in 1879, coincidentally the year my Grandfather was born in London. So at thirty-nine he was no spring chicken to be in the thick of the action. Mind you he had already survived Gallipoli and Jutland so maybe a day trip across the Channel before breakfast, so to speak, was a walk in the park.

At that moment my daydream was brought to an end by a lashing of cold rain against my face as the ship turned quite sharply to starboard to head for the Leopold berth corners of the globe have ever produced. And of course they sold literally hundreds of different makes of cigars, cigarettes and tobacco. An amazing ten metre long mural depicted a square in central Havana, Cuba in a black and white sepia style. I just couldn't take my eyes off it, until the beers arrived anyway. Little squares of cheese arrived too with a supply of wooden cocktail sticks. It reminded me of the Seventies trend of cheese and pineapple on sticks, a 'must have' snack for any party. Today it's steak tartare miniatures, smoked salmon or beluga caviar. How times have changed.

I very quickly discovered that in Bruges when you simply order 'a beer' you are invariably served a local brew called *Jupiler*. It is a Pilsner in effect and jolly refreshing too. Usually served in 'half litres' the beer is pumped into a tall glass until there is a one centimetre collar of white froth on the top and a flat-bladed knife is used to remove any excess before it is offered to the customer. We drank several beers each and there was no sign of a bill arriving at our table. I soon discovered why.

Jerry, the amiable proprietor, came to the table and shook hands with the others first and then me. I think he sensed that I was a non-smoker.

'Yes, Gentlemens, the usual orders?'

I was aghast as carton after carton of Golden Virginia, Old Holburn and other brands seemed to appear from nowhere, conveyed by Jerry's charming wife, Katherine. The prices were ridiculously low by UK standards and, as members of the EU, Brits could take home any quantity they wished so long as it was for personal consumption. How could that possibly be monitored? You tell me! The total tobacco bill for the three smokers was getting on for a thousand pounds. No wonder the beers were 'on the house!'

Carrying much heavier bags than we arrived with (I carried half of Terry's) we headed east towards the main central square. It was probably about mid-day by then and we were feeling peckish, a feeling probably exacerbated by the consumption of beer.

'There it is, the chip shop!' shouted one of the boys. All I could see was a large green wooden shack with a glass counter and serving hatch on one side. It would not have looked out of place at an English village fete selling lemonade and cakes. But this green hut was no ordinary hut. It was reputed to sell the best chips, or Frites as the Belgians call them, in the entire country. Some years later this green hut was to achieve notoriety when it featured on the 'Hairy Bikers' TV Show when the two bearded and affable Geordie foodies paid it a visit.

You didn't have to be a linguistic genius to see that portions were small, medium or large and were served with very generous squirts of mayonnaise or tomato ketchup depending on your taste buds. I decided to exercise caution and ordered a 'medium with mayo' for the price of a Euro from memory. Big mistake! This small mountain of Frites surmounted by a voluminous dollop of mayo gave the impression of a snow-capped Kilimanjaro and I was quite uncomfortable after eating it all I can tell you. A small portion next time maybe to leave room for some more *Jupiler*!

It was round about that time in the square when my feet started to hurt. I don't mean they felt a little tired after the walking. I mean they bloody hurt! Terry had not forewarned me that nearly all of Bruges' streets are cobbled and as bad luck would have it I was wearing shoes with quite thin leather soles. Every step started to hurt. Bugger Bruges! Or should I say bugger Brugge?!

was an exercise I repeated several times over the years while Dad still had the appetite to enjoy them.

So where do the flowers come into this story? Just inside the shop is an escalator going downwards. Step on it and thirty seconds later you will think you are in Covent Garden. The contrast is amazing. Every kind of plant, flower, and shrub you can think of is before you. Smells of seafood are instantly replaced by the scent and bouquets of a thousand flowers. At the far end is an internal waterfall descending some six or seven metres from ground level into a pool just teeming with freshwater fish. Presumably they were for display and effect only and not part of the menu upstairs. I never tired of visiting this shop. My only surprise is that it never seems to have achieved notoriety on the tourist trail.

Leaving the shop and heading towards the town the lake disappears to your right to be replaced by an attractive melange of mostly two storey buildings. Unlike Bruges which is medieval in architectural style, Sluis seemed to be much younger, perhaps only a century old for the most part. The reason for this was only revealed to me when I got into conversation with a friendly English- speaking chap in a coffee shop. He told me that modern Sluis was built by the largely Protestant Dutch as a weekend tourist destination for Catholic Belgians. Visitors by the hundreds would cross over the border for a spot of Dutch 'legover' on Sundays which is why, he further explained to me, you see an amusing combination of businesses today such as a sex shop or a naughty cinema, next door to a family grocers shop. Amazing! Today with the EU and effectively no visible borders, Belgium is probably almost as raunchy and laissez-faire as Holland. But it just goes goes to show what you can find if you dig a little deeper.

Some of the shops almost defy belief. Why, for goodness sake, does Sluis need an 'Australian Ice Cream' shop? Another huge shop was a revelation once you had put your nose inside it. From the window display at street level it looked like a cross between an ornament or glassware shop and a traditional hardware store. Once inside the cavernous interior seemed to go back forever and it was crammed with every kind of kitchenware that you could possibly imagine. As a gift-shop it was invaluable to me on many occasions and over the years I have purchased wine glasses, decanters and simply beautiful crockery decorated with hand painted seafood of every classification and species. I contented myself with some large oval serving dishes decorated with lobsters and crabs. Quite heavy to carry home but worth the effort as I have not seen the like in England – not at those prices anyway.

A favourite shop that sold all manner of cheeses was always on our list to visit. Needless to say that Edam and similar types were the order of the day and many a friend back home was the recipient of the famous 'red ball' as a gift within forty-eight hours or less of purchase. Gift shops also abound in Sluis with local crafts on display and surpisingly many with a maritime or nautical flavour. Initially I found this surprising as Sluis is well inland from the North Sea. On a subsequent visit one reason for this anomaly was at least partially revealed. A huge colourful banner some twenty metres across and several metres deep was stretched across one of the main streets. You did not have to be a language expert to decipher that it was to commemorate '*The Battle of Sluis*' in 1340. The excellent artwork depicted sailing ships and flags I could not immediately recognise. How could a naval battle have taken place in land-locked Sluis? Later and further research revealed that the Battle of Sluis was fought between England and France and essentially marked the commencement of the '100 Year War' between the two countries. King Edward III was determined that France was not to gain the initiative in the Eastern Channel and he threw the kitchen sink at the battle – sink being the operative word. In those days strategic Sluis was on the site of an estuary which became silted up over the centuries. It was a terrible defeat for the French who lost over one hundred and fifty ships and fifteen thousand men as against two ships and some four hundred men on the English side. With results like that is it any wonder the French dislike the Brits so much? Only joking.

You can see Sluis in a whole day even on foot. It is a very pleasant alternative to the crowded streets of Bruges but because you can only reach it by bus or car it is never likely to compete in terms of numbers of tourists. Perhaps for that reason alone you should go out of your way to put it on your itinerary, particularly if you are enjoying a few days in Flanders.

Footnote: As a keen ship spotter I should have recognised the maritime connection with Sluis much sooner than I actually did. The Battle Class of destroyers were built for the Royal Navy in the 1950s and as implied all the vessels were named after famous battles – Trafalgar, Alamein, Agincourt et al. One of the Class was HMS *Sluys* with the pennant number D60.

4.

OSTEND – OOSTENDE

Here we go again with two spellings and pronunciations for the same place. Most of us Brits call it Ostend and the locals call it *"Oostender"* as in the TV show Eastenders. Take your pick. It is one and the same place and any mistake is unlikely to land you in hot water or the wrong place.

To me, Ostend has a charm and character all of its own. I wasn't quite sure what to expect. When I was a young boy my parents used to take trips to Ostend via the ferry from Harwich whilst leaving my sister Linda and I in the safe clutches of grandparents. They were usually away about four or five days so when you take into account that it took all day to drive from Scarborough to Harwich in the family Triumph Mayflower that probably only left two or three days at the most to spend in Flanders. Somewhere in a family photo album is a black and white picture of Mum and Dad with the amazing Ostend Cathedral as a backdrop. This Gothic masterpiece would have dominated the landscape for many miles around when it was first completed in 1908. The casual observer (like me) could be forgiven for thinking that it is much older. More about it later.

As a change from the charms of Sluis, my companion Terry and I decided to visit Ostend, by train this time. A cursory glance at the electronic timetable in Bruges Station informed us that trains departed roughly every half-hour. The next departure was from Vertrep 10 (platform ten). This happened to be the furthest platform away on the concourse but access was easy via an escalator. Be careful not to end up on *Platform Eleven* which is actually a bar and not a platform. Somebody had a sense of humour! I purchased two sets of return tickets blissfully unaware that we could have obtained a 'seniors discount' of about thirty percent for Terry if we had bothered to enquire. So, if you are ever buying tickets on Belgian Railways and you are over sixty-five be sure to ask at the ticket kiosk. If you don't ask you don't get. If you have a UK Senior Railcard then take it with you for good order.

Belgian trains are very punctual as a rule and sure enough this incredibly long and modern train pulled in bang on time. We were slightly confused as all the carriages were double-deckers. So up the stairs we went to hopefully enjoy a better view. We were very impressed with the scale of comfort and we were to find out why before we arrived at Ostend twenty minutes later. The super-smooth train glided almost silently through the north-western suburbs of Bruges past lots of nice Flemish-style houses with smart gardens. A noticeable and unforgettable sight on our left was Bruges High Security Prison. Surrounded by high walls, searchlight towers and even a huge moat filled with green, algae stained water, it looked totally out of place against a backdrop of an otherwise genteel setting. Sadly it is much in demand in these days of terrorism. A decade ago it could have been a work of fiction but today it seems almost a part of everyday life.

The train progressed effortlessly through pretty countryside past many farms, mostly small by British standards I thought. Many dairy cows were visible and I was struck by the number of geese and ducks on seemingly every property. A passion for Foie-Gras perhaps? After about ten minutes the green fields morphed into a more industrial style landscape with a multitude of railway lines appearing out of nowhere and merging into sidings and goods yards. We soon saw small docks, all linked by man-made waterways. There were trains of every description parked in sidings, freight and passenger, and it made you wonder where they all went – or came from.

Just as were slowing to our destination a smiling ticket collector arrived. He clipped our tickets and just said:

'Nexsht time shtay in Shecond Clash please.'

We had no idea that we had inadvertently been travelling First Class! Oh well.

Alighting from the train we were amazed to find that Ostend Railway Station is almost totally surrounded by water. Immediately to our right, just a stone's throw away, was the superstructure of a large ferry with the letters TEF emblazoned on its bright funnel – the logo of Trans European Ferries. Now defunct, the company plied daily between Ramsgate and Ostend. It was a significant reminder that in its heyday Ostend was a terminus for boat trains that could convey you to major European cities as far away as Geneva. Walking along the platform to the main concourse one could see that this huge building had seen better days but its sheer scale and the number of platforms easily betrayed its majestic past and it was easy to imagine hordes of well to do travellers with posh luggage boarding trains bound for Brussels, Berlin and beyond.

Today, Ostend train station is very much geared to commuters heading to Bruges, Brussels and Ghent. Judging from the thousands of bicycles left at the station on a daily basis and the almost complete absence of cars it seems that Ostend residents are amongst the first to 'go green' and show the rest of the world how to do it. The outside of the station was in a poor state of repair – a sad state of affairs for an edifice that was once the gateway to Belgium for so many. Scaffolding had been erected on the front of the station facing the platforms and in fact were bearing witness to the commencement of a major refurbishment programme that would last for over a decade.

After replenishing ourselves with coffees from a temporary 'Portacabin style' refreshment hut we made our way out of the concourse past a 'million' parked bicycles (eat your heart out Beijing) and walked across a narrow road towards what looked like a small boating marina. There were many expensive looking yachts and several catamarans one of which was called *'Hannah'* and we photographed it to show to Terry's granddaughter of the same name. We crossed a narrow road bridge which curiously had traffic lights at both ends. It wasn't until a couple of hours later that we realised that this bridge could open a bit like Tower Bridge in London to let passing marine traffic through. But through to where? It took much further exploration on subsequent visits to discover the answer.

The 'small marina' opened up to a huge expanse of dock that extended several hundred metres right down to the flag-bedecked City Hall. The *Mercator Marina* was named after one Geradus Mercator, a sixteenth century Flemish geographer and cartographer who changed forever the way in which maps were drawn to aid navigation. You might say that what Captain James Cook is to the port of Whitby so is Geradus Mercator to the port of Ostend. His adoration, admiration and even adulation appear to know no bounds in this city. At the head of the marina, moored right outside City Hall, is one of the world's last preserved barquentines named, of course, *Mercator* in his honour. However, the vessel itself was not built in Ostend, nor even Belgium. That honour goes to the Port of Leith in Scotland where is now berthed the Royal Yacht Britannia as a museum ship. Perhaps both City's elders should organise exchange visits. Why not? I digress – again.

Ahead of us and immediately next door to a huge Chinese restaurant we spotted the British Tobacco Shop – a Mecca for smokers like Terry. The shop was busy but the queue inside soon diminished as the affable female staff attended to everybody in turn. Complimentary coffee was available in the shop via a vending machine and using tokens that every customer was given. I love that about the Belgians – they make sure you have a coffee before anything else. Inside the shop was a white cockatoo in a cage. I tried and failed to make conversation with. Perhaps it only spoke Dutch but my efforts amused the staff at the time.

Terry's purchases secured we left the shop and headed left towards what looked like the main promenade. Crossing the road to be on the 'sea side' we went past a restored fishing vessel called the '*Amandine*' (pronounced locally as Amandeener). Set into a dry-dock, it was a visible reminder of the great fishing fleets of yesteryear when hundreds of such vessels operated in the North Sea. It immediately reminded me of the *Hatherleigh,* a Grimsby trawler which was preserved as a museum in Scarborough for many years.

We followed our noses along the promenade towards the fish quay and were surprised to see several memorials to events from World War 2. None was more poignant than a stone tablet dedicated to the Canadian sailors who lost their lives on 14th February 1945 when several vessels of the 29th MTB Flotilla exploded with great loss of life. A wreath of flowers in the shape of the Canadian maple leaf flag lay at the base, perhaps left by a descendant of one of the fallen. On the other hand it might well have been left by a local. The Belgians are very sentimental when it comes to preserving the names of those who came to liberate them. Further along the Promenade was a memorial to Lord Bernard Montgomery.

It all reminded me of a true story concerning an elder brother of my father's, Frank, who at the outbreak of WW2 was training to be a Jesuit priest in Germany and coincidentally working for British Intelligence. Travelling north and then west into the Low Countries, Uncle Frank's last mission was to link up with and escort a junior member of the Belgian aristocracy, a widow with two daughters, onto the last British naval destroyer to leave Ostend before the Germans overran it. They made it! In addition they must have got on very well indeed because they ended up getting married. So the lady became my 'Aunty Mary' by marriage and they ended up retiring to a peaceful life in Banbury Road, Stratford upon Avon. I just wish I had known her maiden and family name as it would be wonderful to make contact with her daughters. All I knew about her family is that they had major connections to SABENA, the Belgian airline.

Eventually we cut back inland down one of many streets running perpendicular to the Promenade. It was obviously market day with a huge square thronged with people, mostly locals shopping, chatting, eating at stalls and drinking coffee. We headed back on a parallel track and eventually emerged right outside the Cathedral, known locally as the

Church of St. Peter and St. Paul. Turning left and then right we spotted the *Amandine* again and several hundred metres away the huge grey shape of Ostend Railway Station.

With one eye on the clock and our returning train to Bruges we decided to leave further exploration for a subsequent trip. Not in a month of Sundays could we have envisaged that another thirty plus visits to this lovely and surprising town would lay ahead of us.

5.

SHIPS & CREW

I mentioned in Chapter One that the ferries from Hull to Zeebrugge are operated by P & O Ferries. I think it is worth telling you a little more about the Company, the ships themselves and the crew.

Mention the single word 'ferry' to me and it immediately conjures up an image of a smallish vessel perhaps twenty to thirty metres long, and used for conveying passengers across a mile or two of water for a duration of ten or twenty minutes at the most. Hong Kong's Star Ferry and Malta's Sliema to Valletta ferries spring immediately to mind. To you it might mean the ferry across the Mersey, the Tyne or even the ferry to the Isle of Wight.

Nothing quite prepared me for my first sight of the mv *Pride of Bruges*. I was at the wheel of my trusty old Volvo 740 (they don't make them like that any more) and we were at the southern end of Ings Lane, Hull heading for King George Dock. Suddenly Terry, mid fag, blurted out:

'There it is. Straight ahead! Look!'

He pointed at the huge blue and white superstructure that was still at least half a mile away. I simply could not believe my eyes. The massive blue funnel added another fifty feet at least to its height. I was mesmerised but instantly recognisable on the funnel was painted the House Flag of P & O. It is one of the maritime world's icons and the four colours – red, yellow, blue and white – depict the national colours of Spain and Portugal, the Iberian Peninsula being the first area the Company plied its trade almost two centuries earlier. Think the *Onedin Line* and think P & O.

Ten minutes later and we had parked the Volvo in P & O's complimentary (in those days) car park and took the short walk into the terminal building. Check-in completed and boarding passes acquired we heading up escalators to the departure lounge and thence onto the huge blue metal boarding gantry. On red deck we were presented with cabin keys and a 'welcome aboard' pack detailing special offers at the Duty Free shop. To be honest all we wanted was a beer in the bar so having dumped our limited luggage in the cabin on green deck we made our way to the Sunset Bar at the very stern of the ship, again on red deck. It was simply teeming with people of every age and description but as schools had started again (it was late January) there were almost no children. We had been amongst the last of hundreds of passengers to board but a heavy 'clunk clunk' every few seconds from below revealed that heavy goods vehicles were still boarding an hour before the due sailing time of 18:30 local time.

'Terry, how many vehicles and passengers does the ship carry?'

'I have no idea, Boy. Ask my namesake the Bar Manager, Mr McMahon. He's been on this ship a few years. He'll be able to tell you.'

I dutifully trotted up to the bar to buy two more pints of excellent Bass bitter. Mr M was most helpful and suggested I pick up a free copy of a Ship's Factsheet which were available at the main desk on the same deck. Now whilst I can quite understand that the majority of paying passengers wouldn't give a fig about the vessel's history and specifications, the difference with me is that when your forbears built the *Titanic* and hundreds of major vessels that plied the trade routes of the world for over a century, one's genes simply itch for information and until that itch is satisfied you are not a happy bunny. That's all I'm saying, OK?

The Fact Sheet did not disappoint. It told me the vessel was built in 1986 by the Japanese NKK yard of Yokohama, Japan. This amused me as I had sailed past that yard on another P & O ship seventeen years before the *Pride of Bruges* had even been launched. When commissioned however, she had been named *Norsun* with the original owners being North Sea Ferries. She had only received her new name a few weeks beforehand when P & O incorporated North Sea Ferries.

The *Pride of Bruges* has a twin ship, the *Pride of York,* but unlike the 'P of B' she was built on the Clyde. It fact she was the last major passenger vessel built on that great river and she was launched by Queen Elizabeth the Queen Mother, also in 1986. Externally the two vessels are almost indistinguishable and only different names and the Ports of Registration on the stern reveal their identity. The *Pride of Bruges i*s registered in Rotterdam and thus flies the Dutch flag. The *Pride of York* was registered in Hull and thus flew the famous 'Red Duster' of the British Merchant Marine. Or at least it did until divisive corporate decisions altered the Port of Registration to Nassau, Bahamas – probably for taxation reasons.

There may have been other thinking in the background behind the decision. In April 1982 Argentina invaded the

British Territory of the Falkland Islands and great swathes of the British Merchant Navy were what was euphemistically called STUFT. This was an acronym for Ships Taken Up From Trade – in other words compulsorily purloined by the Ministry of Defence for war duties. Thus the mv *Norland*, the *Pride of York*'s predecessor was duly 'stuffed' and utilised to convey 2 Para eight thousand miles to the South Atlantic. An old buddy of mine, Rod King, was filling in time as a student as a waiter at the time and amazingly he volunteered to stay on board. Fortunately both he and the *Norland* survived but the Argie Air Force made several attempts to sink her in San Carlos Water. What a tale to tell his grandchildren. Today it would not be possible for a Nassau registered vessel to 'get stuffed' so lets just hope we never have to fight a similar war again.

Anyway back to the storyline. The Sunset Lounge was the main on board venue for entertainment. There is always an 'Entertainments Officer' on board to compere proceedings and introduce the musical entertainment which is usually split into three forty-five minute sessions. It usually, but not always, consists of a male and female duo with one or both playing keyboards or a guitar whilst the other sings. Obviously some are better than others but I can honestly say that overall the standards are very high and I often wonder what happens to them when they complete their ninety days contract or whatever. The biggest surprise often arises when the Entertainments Officer, now in evening dress, suddenly appears at the microphone and morphs into a Shirley Bassey wannabee! Where do P & O find this talent I often wonder? One such lady was a girl called Kirsty Dean who hailed from Aylesbury and I often wonder what happened to her. Another was a tall, slim sensation called Karenina Angelique. She wrote much of her own material and when I asked her where her 'twang' came from she said the audience had to guess. Just before she completed her act very late at night she revealed she came from Brisbane, Queensland but having a 'Pommy Hubby' had lost much of her Strine. She was a real character and was a double for another Aussie, the actress Elizabeth Debicki (Jed) of the Night Manager TV series. Google both of them and you'll see what I mean. I hope Kirsty's and Karenina's fame has increased wherever they are in the world. They sure deserve it.

Perhaps the most memorable act we have ever witnessed was a tribute act to the 'Rat Pack' on the Pride of York in December 2018. Three guys, two white and one black, held us spellbound for a whole hour as they emulated Frank Sinatra, Dean Martin and Sammy Davis Junior. They were absolutely sensational and brought the house down. Mixing with the audience at the bar afterwards they continued their act as if they were still in character. I could have talked to 'Sammy' all night. They were lovely guys too and I would love to see them perform again. They were one of the slickest acts I have ever seen anywhere.

As you might expect with two ferries plying the Hull to Zeebrugge and Zeebrugge to Hull route, one British and one Dutch, the composition of the ships' crews differs markedly. In the reception area on red deck are photos of the ship's Officers and managerial staff. These give you the names of the Master, Chief Officer, Chief Engineer, the Purser, the head of food & beverages etc. So on the *Pride of York* 'Captain Fred Arkwright' (it's nearly always a Yorkshireman) might be accompanied on the list by Andy Nelson, John Smith, Samantha Clark and Alvarro Fernandez. How come? Well an amazing number of the crew have always been

Portuguese. Perhaps this is a historical thing reflecting P & O's pedigree. I'm not sure.

On the Dutch-flagged *Pride of Bruges* you can expect to see a Captain Vandenbroucke, Jerry van Gelder, Martin de Jong, Natalie Rutte etc. filling the same roles.

The only time you really notice any differences are when the Officers make any announcements over the public address system, either just before departures or just prior to arrivals. The difference in styles and voices can be quite amusing – to my sense of humour anyway. As I mentioned in the earlier story '*The Weather Forecast*' the Dutch captains seem to have a measured style, perhaps because they're not speaking in their native tongue, which makes their delivery more listenable and who doesn't admire the linguistic skills of most Dutch-speaking people? The 'bing-bong' of the Tannoy brings almost immediate silence as passengers await the Master's announcement.

'This ish your Captain, shpeaking to you from the bridge' .... etc.

By contrast, a Yorkshire Captain's voice tends to come across as belonging to a friendly pub landlord and often can barely be heard above the clinking of drinks glasses and the general hubub of bar-room chatter.

'Hey ups, This is Captain Arkright on't bridge. We're about ready for off nar, awright? We should be on't berth tomorrow morning about 08:45 'ull time. Forecast's good so enjoy't crossing ..... '

Perhaps it isn't quite like that but if you're a regular passenger on both ships you will soon pick up what I mean about the differences in style. In the course of the evening it is quite common to spot the ship's officers strolling round the various decks and making small talk with passengers. Only once in over sixty trips have I seen a Master at Arms steer a 'worse for wear' passenger towards his cabin. The guy was singing *'On Ilkley Moor bar t'at'* at the top of his voice which probably confused the Dutch officer more than you could possibly imagine.

The two vessels on this route have served P & O and its customers well for many years. I hope that consideration is being given to the acquisition of their replacements. Although both ships have received welcome refits and SLEPS (service life extension programmes) the time will come for new vessels to be purchased. Would it be asking too much to invite what's left of the UK shipbuilding industry to tender for their construction?

6.

ANTWERP

At the time of writing I have only made one single trip to Antwerp. It was a memorable day for a variety of reasons which I will now expand on.

Somewhere on the North Sea between Hull and Zeebrugge my companion Terry said to me:

'I'll tell you what, Boy, just for a change do you fancy going to Antwerp tomorrow instead of Ostend?'

'Sure, why not? Is it easy to get to by train from Bruges?'

'I have no idea. Let's look at the destination board at Bruges station in the morning and take it from there. Another beer?'

And so at about ten o'clock the following morning we found ourselves in the central hall of Bruges Railway Station gazing up at the electronic information board. As you might expect it gave you the name of the destination followed by the time of departure and the number of the platform the train would leave from. The next train to 'Antwerpen' was due to depart in about fifteen minutes time. I purchased the return tickets, making sure that one set was for 'an old person' and after a quick coffee from a kiosk we walked through the busy underpass to take the escalator to the designated platform. We didn't have long to wait and the very long train of at least ten carriages pulled in. It was one of the 'double decker' variety so we climbed upstairs to get a better view.

Travelling roughly south and contrary to our normal north-westerly route to Ostend, the scenery was markedly different as the train meandered gently towards its first major stop – the town of Ghent. From the train window it looked a pleasing and picturesque place but not immediately one that you would jump off at shouting 'I must see this place!' If monasteries and a University don't do it for you then to be honest it's best to carry on to Antwerp.

To date I didn't know a great deal about Antwerp other than the fact that it is the second biggest city in Belgium (after Brussels) and the second biggest port in Europe (after Rotterdam). What I did know, thanks to Terry's almost fanatical quest for war knowledge, was that Antwerp got hit by more V1 'Doodlebug' rockets than did London. Amazing but true. Such were Hitler's efforts to stop the Allies taking control of the Port of Antwerp, what was left of the V1 armoury was thrown at the city. Needless to say civilian casualties were horrendous as this 'fire and forget' weapon was not discriminatory in who or what it destroyed. The shipyards were a major casualty too which reminded me that two of P & O's passenger-cargo liners, the *Cathay* and the *Chitral*, were constructed in Antwerp. Both vessels were regular sights when I lived in the Far East.

It took about an hour and a quarter to reach our destination as our long train pulled into Antwerp Station. I had read that it had undergone a massive and expensive restoration programme but the vista that lay before us was truly amazing. Think St. Pancras, London then double it! We alighted from the train both of us keen to satisfy two human needs. Terry needed a fag and I needed a pee. I spotted a sign for WCs and also a Tourist Information desk where I could hopefully obtain a street map. I pointed Terry to the main exit where he could have a smoke and almost in passing said to him:

'And mind that hooker over there. She's touting for business....'

By his nonchalant shrug of the shoulders I was not sure if he believed me or not. Five minutes later, post pee and having also acquired a map, I rendezvoused with Terry outside the station.

'By God, you were right. She was a hooker!'

'I bloody told you. How much did she want?'

'Fifty Euros, but I politely declined!'

'I should think so too. Buy me a beer and I promise I won't tell Mae (Terry's wife) about your little encounter.'

'Deal! Come along, Boy. Let's head this way. Where's that map?'

After the hooker the first human we spotted was what could only have been a scruffy looking Eastern European woman, possibly Roma, nestling twin bairns one at each breast. Surrounded by carrier bags of possessions she was in stark contrast to the opulence that greeted us within just a hundred metres. Diamond shop after diamond shop, one after the other, their sparkling displays making it look like Christmas had come early, although it was only early October. I had never seen so many carats in my life, not even in the plushest and richest streets of down-town Hong Kong. Some were so big the carats morphed into turnips! It started to drizzle.

I immediately cast my mind back to the opening chapters of Frederick Forsyth's novel *The Fourth Protocol* and an Antwerp diamond merchant who got caught up in espionage. Although not as famous as *The day of the Jackal* I still regard it as his best work. No matter. We carried on regardless despite the rain which was becoming increasingly tiresome. Terry habitually wears a cap, I don't.

'Raindrops keep falling on my head' didn't really do it for me in *Butch Cassidy and the Sundance Kid* and it certainly wasn't doing it for me on the streets of 'Antwerpen.' I had soon had enough!

'Terry, there's a nice friendly looking bar across the road. Let's take shelter and refreshment until the weather improves shall we?'

Terry didn't say anything but dutifully crossed the road and stuck his head briefly inside.

'You're right, Boy! It is a friendly place. That was Terryspeak for 'Smoking Allowed.' All was well with the world for the next hour, then the next one. The weather did not improve and neither of us were equipped to cope with it.

'Tell you what, Boy, now we've got our Antwerp bearings why don't we come back again another day? If we get the next train back to Bruges we'll have time for a few at the station before we get back on the coach to Zeebrugge.'

How could I refuse? And so ended our first and only trip to Antwerp. We hadn't seen the famous Zoo, the docks or a single VI bomb sight. Just thousands of diamonds and the inside of a single bar. Oh yes, and a hooker!

Footnote: Just two months before writing this tale I attended the funeral service of a former colleague of my father, one Paul Royen. I had known Paul was Belgian by birth but I was staggered to learn from the Eulogy that he was born in Antwerp and had escaped to England on a British warship just prior to the German invasion in 1940. In that he had something in common with my Uncle Frank as I revealed earlier in Ostend – Oostende. Why do we only learn so much about good people when they're gone?

7.

WIPERS

We British call it 'Wipers,' the French call it Ypres and the Dutch-speaking Belgians call it Ieper (pronounced Eeper). Either way we are all referring to that small town in the extreme south-west of Flanders that gained eternal notoriety for the role it played in World War One. A visit to 'Wipers' is almost regarded as a pilgrimage by many who lost forbears in the horrendous battles that took place in the vicinity of this once prosperous medieval cloth town. In 1914 it found itself just to the west of the front line, the Ypres Salient, and was demolished by shelling over the next four years.

So, we made the decision to visit Ypres and in particular the Menin Gate where are inscribed the names of tens of thousands of fallen soldiers with no known graves. The trip would take rather more planning than the usual foray to Ostend and necessitated an overnight stay at a nice B & B conveniently sited just a few hundred metres from Bruges Railway Station. We checked-in within half an hour of leaving the Albion Tours coach and the friendly proprietress told us we could leave our bags in the room despite the early hour.

Once inside the station proper I ventured forth to the ticket counter to purchase return tickets and made enquiries for the best route. There is only one 'best route to Ieper' it seemed and that was via another town called Kortrijk ("core trick") where we would have to change trains and possibly wait quite a while for a connection. In addition the second train would not, it seemed, go straight to Ieper but via another small town called Poperinge. The correct pronunciation eluded me.

So, our train headed south-east at first seemingly taking the track to Ghent and thence Brussels but seemed to turn smartly to the right and headed south. We were only a couple of weeks away from the winter solstice and the milky sunshine at midday was the only indication of our geographical heading. The land lost its flatness and the topography became more undulating. The countryside took on a new character and to my mind at least it started to lose the charm of flat wetlands and canals so typical of the Flanders we had become so used to. The train was in no hurry and made several stops before we reached Kortrijk which, from the train at least, appeared quite a sizeable town. Prior reading-up revealed that Groeninge, near Kortrijk had been the site of the famous Battle of the Golden Spurs in 1302. Flemish troops, ably supported by thousands of workers across many industries, rose up against their French Lords and Masters and heavily defeated them. The 'golden spurs' were war trophies and were exhibited for years until the French recovered them in 1380. It was an important moment in Flemish history and still to this day goes some way to explaining the antipathy between the Dutch and French speaking communities.

The train for Poperinge arrived on a different platform in another part of the sizeable station and we were amused by the very low level of the platform. It was as though it had been built for a much smaller and lower train. Perhaps it had! A World War One troop train maybe? We were relieved to see a guard trot along with a pair of folding stepladders so that we could actually climb onto the carriage. It was quite a while before the train started to move and another half-hour before we reached Poperinge and we'd still not see hide nor hair of Ieper although the guard had assured us in excellent English that we were definitely on the right train. With Ieper being geographically roughly between Kortrijk and Poperinge we had assumed the train would stop at Ieper first. Wrong! In an oddly circuitous route it went to Poperinge first like a giant train set before turning back to Ieper. We got off (at a normal sized platform) and exited the Station. It was lunchtime and we both needed a beer and a snack of some kind.

We headed east towards the town centre and I was surprised how modern many of the buildings were but somehow they did not seem out of place against much older traditionally styled edifices. Had the new buildings been replacements for those obliterated in times of war? A smart road of modern shops gave way to an open square which revealed the magnificently restored Ypres Cathedral on our left. You could immediately see the change and coloration in the brickwork between the older and lower sections of the building that had survived the shelling and the upper vantages that had replaced the fallen sections. It was very, very impressive.

We found the *'Over the Top'* café and partook of beer, coffee, croque monsieur sandwiches and a bowl of frites, the latter being an almost compulsory accompaniment to any Flemish snack. It was a cool day to say the least and the warm food revived us. The helpful young waitress pointed us in the direction of the Menin Gate which had been the main attraction and reason for our convoluted journey. It was, she said, only a few minutes walk away. The word Gate is a bit of a misnomer to say the least. Forget garden gates or five-bar gates leading to a field of sheep. This type of Gate refers to the ancient and medieval Gates of a town or city to guard against invasion by those who wish to perpetrate evil against you.

Thus the Menin Gate is actually a massive stone arch that towers over the main road into the town from the eastern end. The road is single carriageway and traffic is controlled by lights at either end. It took us both by surprise as when you see it on TV, perhaps on Armistice Day, the camera angles cannot do justice to the sheer scale of the structure. Gazing heavenwards reveals giant glass skylights to allow for sun and natural light but what hits you immediately are the names engraved on the walls. Thousands and thousands of names. And they all have one thing in common – they all died and have no known graves. It is truly humbling and inspiring, even in the silence of mid-afternoon in mid-winter. We could only imagine what it must feel like at eight o'clock every evening when, without fail, the Last Post is played by a detachment of the Belgian Fire Brigade. One day I will go back to listen to it.

We were just on the point of leaving and walking back to the town centre when a middle-aged gentleman, obviously a local, rang the bell on his bicycle and slowed to a halt alongside us.

'Are you folks first time visitors?' We nodded and replied that indeed we were.

'If you're looking for a particular name then let me help you. Here, follow me.'

We walked only a short distance, maybe twenty metres, to what resembled a small door in the stone wall. The door was about a metre off the ground and looked rather like the metal door of a small office safe with a simple handle on it. The gentleman opened it and swung it open. Inside were about a dozen heavy looking binders and he picked out one at random.

'In these books are listed the names in alphabetical order of every single name inscribed on the Menin Gate and it tells you on which panel you can find the name.'

As it happened we weren't looking for a particular name but anyone reading this story might find this bit of information useful, to say the least. What a nice, friendly chap he was too. It being Monday it was a very quiet day and the 'In Flanders Fields' museum was closed, the window displays just hinting at the memorabilia and exhibits within. We resolved to return another time, perhaps in the summer and definitely not on a Monday.

The return journey to Bruges, via Kortrijk, was baffling as this time we appeared to pass through Poperinge twice. Somebody was having a laugh with the train set!

Before closing this story I must tell you of the inscription carved in stone beneath the British Lion reposing on the very top of the Gate at the eastern entrance:

**TO THE ARMIES
OF THE BRITISH EMPIRE
WHO STOOD HERE
FROM 1914 TO 1918
AND TO THOSE OF THEIR DEAD
WHO HAVE NO KNOWN GRAVE**

These are solemn words that you would normally expect to see in a Commonwealth War Graves cemetery in some far-flung post of Empire like Hong Kong, India or Singapore. You do not expect to see them less than a hundred miles from our nation's capital, London.

The Belgians look after the memory of our fallen as if they were their own. For that reason alone I think it should be incumbent upon every true Brit to visit the Menin Gate and the charming little town we have come to call 'Wipers.' Spend the day there and a few quid – or even a few Euros – your visit will be really appreciated. Like my father had reminded me before I even set foot on Flanders' soil:

> 'We Brits have a special relationship with the Belgians, Boy.'

8.

THE TRAM RIDE

We had heard a lot about 'that tram' that runs up and down the Belgian coast very close to the edge of the North Sea. Featured on numerous TV travel programmes it struck me as being one of those 'must do' things. For some reason we Brits seem to have a thing about trams. Most major cities were served by trams. Initially horse-drawn, then steam powered and finally all-electric, they were major contributors to the growth of major conurbations like Liverpool, Newcastle and Glasgow. One of the most memorable auto-biographies I have ever read was called *'Listening for a Midnight Tram'* written by the famous newspaper editor Sir John Junor who laid awake at night until he heard the reassuring clunk of the tram that he knew was bringing his mother home from her night-time cleaning job at a Glasgow cinema. Today, those trams that still run remind us of a bygone age when owning cars was the prerogative of the rich.

The Belgian Coastal Tram ("the Kusttram") is something of an exception to the rule in that it runs entirely along a length of coastline from Knokke-Heist in the north near the Dutch border, to De Panne in the south near the French border. Its sole purpose is to link all the coastal communities together and it makes no pretensions to do anything else. You cannot access it from anywhere other than on the coast so first of all you have to reach one of the dozens of stations which it serves. Believe it or not it has been in operation since 1885 and although it has been operated by regional governments from time to time, today it is managed and operated by the De Lijn Co. whose purple and yellow logo is a familiar sight to all bus-users in Bruges.

For the technically minded the Kusttram is all-electric (always has been) and operates at 600v DC running on a 1,000 mm gauge track via overhead powered cables. On its forty-five mile (70km) length are many pedestrian crossing points, hence the overhead cables and not a third 'live' rail which would have fried many a poodle and doubtless a few people too.

Dwelling on the idea of taking the tram-ride for years we had spotted the trams from time to time on other excursions but not being locals were uncertain where to actually board one. The final completion of Ostend's Railway Station refurbishment gave birth to a brand new Train/Coach/Tram interchange so after making enquires on one particular visit to Ostend we decided that on the next trip we would not take the coach from Zeebrugge to Bruges but would go straight to Ostend and 'do the tram.' Thus by ten o'clock on the day of travel we went to the ticket office of the Kustttram and made enquiries. The helpful ticket attendant, a young male student doing a holiday job for the summer, explained that to do the whole route in a day was far too ambitious.

'You will never make it up and down in one day. I recommend you head south towards the French border, get off for some lunch around mid-day and then come back. On another day you can take the tram north to the Dutch border via Zeebrugge and Blankenberg.'

It was sound advice so we took it, buying two return tickets for 'old people' at a very reasonable price of about five Euros each from memory.

'Make sure you get on the tram going south to De Panne – that one there!' He pointed.

Perhaps he was used to crazy Brits waiting on the wrong side of the track and going the wrong way. Easily done. With a cheery wave we hopped onto the green three-carriage tram. We didn't have long to wait and our carriage was only about half-full. We pulled out of the depot and headed for the Mercator Marina passing down the entire length of it on the south and eastern sides. There were many stops in the city before we finally emerged into less built up areas but eventually the North Sea emerged on our starboard flank, so to speak, with buildings largely confined to landward. Sadly the weather, which had not looked particularly promising since dawn, took a turn for the worse and a damp mist curled in from the North Sea like a 'Haa' or a 'Fret' as we call them in Yorkshire. This did not augur well and before long a steady drizzle had set in.

Two local 'scroats' aged about thirty had boarded our carriage at the last of the 'city stops' and they slurped wine from green bottles as they slurred at each other in Dutch. They had a whippet on a lead which they kicked under the bench seats. A smart French-speaking lady got on and immediately started to remonstrate with them. She didn't speak Dutch and they didn't speak French. My 'O' level French (unused since Montreal in 1969) told me that unless they quit drinking she would report them. They got the message and put the wine away. The lady turned to me and smiled. She didn't speak a single word of English either but eventually I garnered enough fourth form French to tell her that we were hoping to get to De Panne for some lunch. In the event we did not get that far. It had mercifully stopped raining and we alighted the tram at a place called 'Newport Bad' (I kid you not) and made enquiries at the ticket office as to where we might obtain some coffee and lunch.

We were out of luck! The helpful English-speaking attendant told us that the summer season hadn't got going yet and with the bad weather we would be lucky to find anywhere open. However she pointed us in the right direction for the seafront and we looked forward to some fresh air after the steamed-up and claustrophobic atmosphere on the tram. A short two hundred metre walk brought us to the water's edge and a promenade that seemed to stretch for ever. The buildings were an odd mix of the very new and the very old, the latter being timber framed structures of an almost medieval appearance. They all had one thing in common. They were all shut. After walking for perhaps five hundred metres along the seafront we gave up looking for a coffee shop and headed back towards the Tram Stop. Clearly it wasn't our day. It was hard to believe that just a few weeks later the whole place would be absolutely teeming with thousands of holidaymakers drinking beer, eating waffles and frites and generally enjoying their version of 'the seaside.' It is very different to Brighton, Blackpool or Bridlington but to native Belgians it is their summer playground and they just love it!

We took the Tram back to Ostend arriving adjacent to the Mercator Marina about one o'clock. It was raining heavily and we took refuge, beer and lunch in a nice café with an outside smoking area that, thankfully, was protected with a huge waterproof awning. The waitress, Zoe, was absolutely charming and went to great pains to find us a table that was 'drip free' from the now torrential rain. The café itself was part of the Burlington Hotel complex and I decided to make enquiries about a possible future stay.

After delivering my default dish of 'spag bol' and Terry's ham omelette and frites, Zoe suggested that we made enquiries at the hotel's reception desk immediately next door. We didn't have long to wait as before we had even finished eating a pleasant thirty-something lady emerged from the door obviously on a 'fag break' from her duties. Sadly for her despite many clickings her lighter refused to ignite. She glanced hopefully in Terry's direction, the curling smoke from his roll-up revealing his similar pleasure. Terry grinned and passed me his lighter to hand to her through a gap in the plastic awning.

'Hello, thank you very much! My name is Katrien. Would you like details of the hotel's tariffs? If you do just pop into reception next door and I'll give you a welcome pack with details.'

So I did just that. She told me that Ostend was her home-town, born and bred, and that if we ever came as guests to the hotel she would be pleased to advise us on points and places of interest. Now without wishing to knock my fellow countrymen I just cannot imagine many bilingual receptionists in Bridlington offering the same service to a visitor from Flanders who wanders up the Yorkshire coast after disembarking the ferry at Hull. Just saying.

The "Kusttram" was an adventure, albeit an uncompleted one. Next time, I am sure, it will be an overnight (or two) stay at the Burlington Hotel and the tram-ride north to Knokke-Heist.

At the time of writing the Belgian Coastal Tram is the longest in the world. Well I did tell you that Belgium is a surprising place.

9.

FOOD & DRINK

Ask your average Brit to shout out the first word that comes into their head when you say the word 'Belgium' and I'm willing to bet that the vast majority today will say chocolates! Certainly most females would give that answer. It might make a good question for that quiz show "Pointless" where a low score would be achieved by 'rifles' for many ex-servicemen who lament the passing of the Belgian FN rifle as standard Army issue.

But it is easy to see why chocolates is the popular answer. Chocolate shops are simply everywhere, certainly in the town of Bruges. Now I don't have a sweet tooth but unfortunately most of my female friends do. I say unfortunately because every time I announce I am going to make another trip I am bombarded with requests.

'Ooh Mark, can you bring me some of those cherry chocolates? You know the ones I mean – with the stone still in and the stalk still attached.'

'Can you get me a pair of dark chocolate boobies as a joke pressie for my Grandad? He's eighty next week and you know what a sense of humour he has. Or white chocolate if they don't have dark and yes, while you're there can you ….?'

I think it was on about my third trip that I decided to find one shop where I could satisfy all the requests in one fell swoop – a 'one stop' chocolate shop if you like. I found a family-owned shop called *Verheecke* on Steenstraat roughly mid-way between Simon Stevin Plein and the main dominant square in the town centre. You can't miss it as it has an eye-catching dark red canopy across its frontage. Here you can buy every kind of chocolate product you like. The product range is immense and it seems that nothing is so unusual that it cannot be manufactured from chocolate. Thus you can buy chocolate male and female genitalia, lobsters, fish, animals and even nuts and bolts. Bizarre but true. Take a look for yourself.

In the run-up to Christmas and Easter I would take the opportunity to buy maybe ten small boxes of assorted 'house chocolates' as gifts. The neat box with a red ribbon and a foreign name '*Verheecke*' with a Brugge address and label in the house colours, lending an authentic touch to a small but appreciated gesture. There are many such retail outlets of course but I always found this family-owned business extremely obliging over many years with the same people serving you on almost every occasion.

Chocolate apart, Belgium is famous for its beers – not just the taste but the sheer number of breweries in the country, over four hundred in all. I once pointed out to an Australian taxi driver who was boasting about his country's 'world-beating consumption' that it fact it was tiny Belgium who had the world's highest per capita consumption at over a hundred litres per year. He was not impressed I can tell you. Of other places I have visited the only other city that came close to rivalling Bruges in the beer department was Cincinnati, Ohio. Thousands of immigrant Germans had turned the city into the 'Munchen of the Midwest' where a beer called *Christian Moerlein* is the equivalent of the ubiquitous Jupiler. In addition to Jupiler the visitor will come across brand names such as Duvel, Chimay (a Trappist ale) and Kwak (think of ducks) but be warned, do not imbibe too much of the latter as it has a very high alcohol content. You don't want to be 'quacking' all the way home. The best-selling Stella Artois is perhaps the best known Belgian beer as it has been widely exported for decades and is a familiar brand here in the UK, its popularity aided no doubt by sporting event sponsorship over many years. I am not a fan of blonde or yellow beers, sometimes called wheat beers or Blanche beers, but if you are then any friendly bartender will help you choose one. Hoegarden is so named after the town in which it is brewed.

I have already mentioned Belgium's famous Frites which no first time visitor to Bruges must ignore. I don't know why they taste different to the chips we have with our cod or haddock but I'm telling you, they just do! Perhaps it is the variety of the potato that is grown in Flanders soil, the way they are cooked or the oil they are fried in. I just don't know. Perhaps it is a combination of all three. I have personally grown many varieties of potatoes over the years and I would love to know the answers.

But what do the locals eat with their darling Frites? Well they are particularly fond of their own home-reared beef. My late grandfather took me as a small boy to many a cattle show and one strain I especially remember was the Belgian Blue, a hybrid originally nurtured in Liege and admired for its high muscle/fat ratio. The locals have a penchant for barely cooked or even raw beef dishes such as steak tartare, often called by its alternative name of steak Américain. Belgian beef stew is also popular with cubes of the leanest braised steak served in a rich red wine gravy – always served with Frites of course. Mashed potato is simply unheard of so do not embarrass yourself by asking for it.

Also, you cannot visit Bruges, or indeed anywhere in Flanders, without trying the moules – mussels to you and me. Steamed with small onions and white wine and served, of course with Frites, they are simply exquisite. All washed down, needless to say, with a half-litre (or two) of local beer. For a small country with only a forty mile coastline the Belgians use their proximity to the North Sea with gusto. In addition to moules other shellfish like lobster, langoustine, and oysters are ever popular. Another speciality is called 'anguille au vert' consisting of large pieces of eel cooked with masses of green herbs. My father would have been in his element!

If you have a sweet tooth then the scores of cake shops and patisserie will leave mouth-watering impressions on you. Likewise the eye-catching cheese shops cannot escape your attention. Ask the shopkeeper for a recommendation if you are uncertain of your selection and don't forget to take a big vacuum-packed chunk home as a gift. If you're looking for something a bit different why not try some Passendale, a soft light cheese with lots of holes in from Western Flanders. A sort of holy Camembert!

As for cafés and restaurants the choices before you are mind boggling. As a foodie myself I have discovered some absolute gems down side streets slightly off the beaten track. Explore for yourself and don't be afraid to ask a local. If you're staying overnight then I offer a word of caution. If you spot a good venue at lunchtime and think 'we'll come back tonight' then just check it is open in the evening first. More than once I have been caught out and left disappointed. I can thoroughly recommend 'Poules Moules' (The Chicken and Mussels) in Simon Stevin Plein just a stone's throw from Jerry's Cigar Bar if time is not on your side and it's your first visit. (Square 4F on the Insight map of Bruges).

There is something for everybody and of every sized pocket whether it's some tasty 'street food' or a sit-down five star gourmet restaurant. Belgians love their food and they would like you to enjoy it too. Just trust me on that one. Well, I won't waffle on any longer on this section but that reminds me – do try the local waffles!

10.

COME BACK AGAIN

Not in my wildest dreams on my first trip from Hull to Zeebrugge could I have ever imagined that over almost the next two decades would I make over sixty such trips. My images of Belgium as a flat, boring almost desolate wetland had been totally dispelled by reality.

In the foregoing Tales I have, I hope, given you more than a little inkling of what to expect. They are not tourist guides or travelogues. You can buy one of those if needs must. There are plenty to choose from. However, I do recommend that you buy a good map and my choice would be the *Insight/Fleximap* of Bruges which you can buy in WH Smiths or online for around a fiver. It also offers a small scale map of West Flanders so you can get your bearings from the whole coastline and you too can plan your excursion on that famous "Kusttram." The small but useful insertion of a street map of Ypres is also an advantage should you take my advice and spend a day on a visit to "Wipers."

I have written about Ostend, Sluis, Ypres and Antwerp as destinations easily reached from Bruges by train, bus or tram. So why haven't I gone into the same detail with Bruges which is your normal dropping off point when you arrive by sea from the Port of Zeebrugge? The answer is quite simple – you need to explore this lovely city for yourself. Buy the map I mention above and just follow your nose. That's what I did for the first dozen trips.

Your first visit is likely to afford you only seven hours of 'tourist time' as it were. Spend it wisely. Do not try to 'do Bruges' in a day like some brain-dead lemming following a tourist guide with a flag on a stick. They are everywhere in Bruges and you can spot them on every single day except Christmas Day. From the normal coach drop-off point at the 'Bargeplein' (square 5J on the Insight map) you essentially have two choices. You can walk north over an almost Oriental looking decorative bridge across a lake towards the spires of the town centre. It's less than a mile (in our money) and will take you past many old streets and squares until you reach the Belfort (the Belfry) made famous in the movie *In Bruges* when someone fell from it. Or, departing Bargeplein, you can walk left (west) and follow the main road as it curves round towards Bruges Railway Station which you simply cannot miss. This is your first objective if you wish to venture to any of the four above-mentioned destinations.

If at the end of your excursion and on your return to Bruges you are in need of liquid refreshment, then I heartily recommend the Jean Max Bar which is hidden out of immediate sight behind the book shop and estate agents on your right hand side as you exit the station. It has an inside bar and a pleasant seating area outside. If the weather should be inclement they will switch on the overhead patio heaters to ward off the chill. Oh yes, and if you ask nicely, the proprietress will pour you a small complimentary glass of the finest 'egg-nog' I have ever tasted anywhere. On a shelf above the bar inside is an amazing collection of Belgian

Railways hats, mostly an orange colour, and sporting the big encircled letter 'B' of the company's logo. I tried, without success, to buy one as a birthday gift for Terry who just loves his collection of caps. I think I'll have to bribe a member of the Railways staff one day.

I couldn't possibly within these ten Tales give you a complete account of all the places I have seen and people I have met in this amazing town. You will have to discover and explore it for yourself. Talk to people on the buses, on the trains and in the shops. Venture into as many cafés and coffee shops as your fancy takes you. It won't break the bank. Ask the waiters and waitresses their names and remember them for next time. I guarantee you one thing – if you do, they will remember you.

If, as I predict, your first visit simply serves to whet your appetite for future trips, then you might like to consider a couple of nights in a hotel. Just Google Bruges Hotels and the choice before you is amazing from brand-new budget accommodation to older style family-owned establishments. I particularly like the *Karos* (Carriage) Hotel which is older and has an air of tranquillity about it, the miniature carriage in the foyer lending an almost aristocratic ambience. You can find it about five hundred yards north of the 'Fountain Square' near the concert hall on the main road to Zeebrugge. (Square 3F). But make your own mind up. Like I said, the choice is huge and with Bruges being an all-year-round destination you cannot fail to find accommodation to suit your own taste and pocket.

I mentioned earlier that we once fell foul of the Immigration Officers at the Port of Zeebrugge. It was most unexpected and this is what happened.

Terry decided to treat his two young grandsons to a trip to Bruges one half-term. We checked in as usual at the Port of Hull and enjoyed an event-free crossing. All went well until the lads, Finlay and Lewis (14 and 12) presented their passports to the Immigration Officers. Almost immediately Terry and the boys were apprehended and steered into an interview room. Unaware of this potential disaster I had already 'gone through' and was heading for the escalators and the exit lobby two levels beneath.

It was twenty minutes before the three of them emerged, all sporting huge grins of relief. I asked what the problem had been.

'You won't believe this. The boys have different surnames to me as they have their father's family name. They believed there was a possibility that their mother had 'exported' her sons amid divorce proceedings, possibly in contravention of a court order. We should have brought a letter signed by her giving permission for her sons to leave the country.'

'So what happens now?'

'As their temporary guardian I had to sign a legal document promising to return them to the ferry by six o' clock tonight lest Interpol would issue a Europe-wide warrant for my arrest!'

The twenty minute wait had afforded me the opportunity to go 'ship spotting' around the fabulous collection of models on display, all mounted within glass cases. They are a potted history of P & O Ferries and its immediate predecessor, North Sea Ferries. I never tire of gazing at them. My favourite is a model of the mv *Norwind* built in Bremerhaven in 1966. The vessel was only a hundred metres long and some three thousand tons displacement – that's a lot smaller than a present day *Daring* Class destroyer. If you know your ships like I do, you can't help but observe that the *Norwind* is like a miniature ss *Canberra*, an eminent and classic liner from the P & O stable of yesteryear and, like the previously mentioned *Norland*, a veteran of the Falklands campaign. The twin side-by-side buff funnels caused a sensation when she emerged from the slipway at Harland and Wolff's yard in Belfast in 1960. The design obviously caught another naval architect's eye as well.

Nobody knows what the future holds for the ferries that daily ply between the great Ports of Hull and Zeebrugge. I can tell you something though. They have changed and enriched my life immeasurably and taught me a lot about that 'little country across the North Sea' who have been our friends and allies for over a century.